Kicking stigma
Charlotte Rameka

If you have read my writing, you would know that I like to get my readers to think about curiosity because how can you possibly open your mind to something new without it. Opening yourself and your mind allows you to gain an informed opinion, more knowledge, and a variety of viewpoints. Opening your heart and mind is hard but essential to get rid of the dust you call the unknown.

Who are we to decide who someone will become and their place in the world being and individual with self-orientated goals is perfectly normal? They may also not look the same as yours and that is okay. astounds me that people have the audacity to determine someone else's future or withheld there potential or desire for what they want to accomplish in their life.

But now I ask you to open your hearts to suicidal ideation this might just save one of your loved ones from doing something they cannot take back.

Suicidal ideation

Suicidal ideation is a very serious underlying symptom of any illness but most common depression. It can totally flip the perception that someone has of themselves which drive people to attempt or commit suicide. Suicide ideation is also often a symptom of feeling trapped like there's no way out. Now I am not going to hide behind the stigma and use a different word because how are we supposed to make a change if we can't even acknowledge the problem. Suicide is a person's escape to the thing they don't want to feel to something they don't want to remember to something they no longer can cope with they want it all to stop!

But it doesn't

I am telling you this from the most genuine part of my soul that I have attempted and lost multiple people to suicide. I know the pain all too well to say it doesn't stop by suicide.

Let's take a break pace ourselves

"you are not the darkness you have endured. You are the light that refuses to surrender"
John mark green

Stigma is such a life of its own it festers on society's viewpoints, but does this mean it right?

Dear society

Think of it as a broken ankle. To me I think about a broken ankle its inflamed tissue and muscles its swollen ligaments and skin how the ability to walk is now impaired. Then I think about Response to trauma, unhealed trauma responses create dysregulation in mood. It makes it hard to maintain healthy relationships, struggle with impulses not only self-harm and has a narrow-tunneled mind that was created by trauma. Rejection is also felt a lot more intensely then normal both being a significant event, but one largely ignored. That makes me curious. As a society we need to become a lot more openminded to things we haven't been through and see that people experience life differently to what you or I do and that that is very valid. You might not always see the unwellness, but it is there and if we only opened our hearts and minds, people would feel more comfortable about speaking out. Its impossible to save every single person but every person deserves the chance to be saved. People deserve to be treated with dignity and respect no matter the choices they have made I feel strongly on this point.

Labeling

In human nature we tend so see a problem then label it to find a solution. This is the way we can problem solve to find ways to deal and cope and learn to manage our mental health. This can be helpful to show insight to what we are experiencing but labeling come with negative things also. It can make people feel like they are put in a box. That they are now deemed different this is not true. Yes, the thought processes are different, but we are all human beings, and we all have goals and aspirations. I think people forget that what life looks like for one person is different to the other and that that doesn't make us different in fact how we treat people makes us more different. People who degrade people are nasty and it is not okay you have no idea of what someone has been through and how it affects them, we all deal with hardships in different ways. Life throws curveballs in everyone lives it just looks different.

Triggers

This can be something in the environment that sets off the thought or feeling within yourself. This could be a smell, the detail of surroundings, color, a phrase, this is only to name a few. Could be a memory or special day. I can't stress this enough sometimes there are triggers and sometimes they are concious sometimes they are not. Triggers form an uncomfortable feeling that sometimes people feel they cannot escape. It can create a pain people feel will never stop. To help people understand it triggers can also be positive if you think about a pet for example if someone loves dogs and drives past a couple walking a dog it can send messages to the brain of joy. This can make someone feel happy. Now if you stay with me, when someone sees the colour red they can associate it with blood then associate it with a blood test or needle this causes uncomfortable feelings and fear. This is very real for the person/individual. This can present in many forms. People who already suffer trauma find it anxiety provoking to live life normally because of the risk of getting re traumatized by triggers. Triggers can lead to suicide attempts as the person is looking for a back door which you might not be able to grasp but believe me some things are extremely scary to face and some people do not tolerate the pain. The feeling of not being able to move past something can be daunting like things will never end. At times for me the pain felt so unbelievably painful I felt if I was to put that on to someone then they would feel that pain too I didn't want that, I was blind. But to be open and honest that made things so much worse. It made me accountable I was defiantly not ready for that. Because my triggers affect me significantly, I would avoid situations like talking about feelings and what was going on in my head and nod my head to scared to stand up for myself. I thought people would be happier if I just agreed to what's being said but instead no one knew how I truly felt this is such a lonely way to be. It made sense in my head, but it done me no favors. I was often misunderstood. Always felt not heard.

Isolating

This is a significant indicator that something isn't right. Withdrawing from things people Normally do is a sign that something is going on. Isolating can be people's way to slip away unnoticed as they feel that if the become alone its easier to act on what they feel. Also, it eventually reinforces what they believe which is that they are alone and by themselves. But this is very not true. Sometimes people isolate due to false beliefs of themselves or due to comments they have ruminating on. A way to notice that someone it is isolating is they withdrawing from there normal activities, no longer getting enjoyment out of everyday activities, and cancelling plans last minute. I've noticed within myself and others around me that when I isolate doing things become extremely overwhelming because isolating has become a safety net in my mind, but it has made me conform to isolation.

To Reader

Thank you for reading what you have so far I know the things you have read are not easy to digest. I acknowledge the time you are spending to read this and be curious about what you will read next. Take a break when you need and read at your own pace. Warning that the next section may make you feel venerable or overwhelmed. Sometimes books can be educational but also exhausting so just know your limits and remember that you are important. I will catch up with you later in the book.

Putting on a front

Sometimes as humans we put on a front so that other people do not see our pain, frustration, how upset we are and distress. In fact I can guarantee you that in some point of your life you have done this weather its to stop others in seeing you pain, to stop an argument progressing, to not make a situation worse, to avoid drama and many more reasons. But sometimes people become so controlled by how they think and feel that they completely shut out the world and continue on like they aren't suffering when they are, and this becomes very detrimental to the person mental health and is a unfortunate sign that no one sees of suicidal ideation. Before I was able to communicate my distress this is exactly what I did. But I did it because I didn't know how to express my thoughts and feelings in a healthy way. I didn't want to burden people with my feelings and simply didn't know how to ask for help. If I can look back on this, I wish I knew how to communicate or simply say I am struggling and talk to the right people about my distress. I made many mistakes and still make mistakes, but I now try to tell the right people what I am going through. Honestly, I am still stubborn but as my therapy continues, I am learning to notice my mistakes and learn from them. The process isn't always quick but learning to notice and acknowledge your feeling is first step.

"just because no one else can heal or do your inner work for you does not mean you need to do it alone"
Lisa ollvera, 2022

Expectation

Why are we so hard on others? Why do we judge something we haven't walked through or lived? and are we different?

See there is no quick answers to that question because human beings are not easy to understand, and I quite frankly don't understand Why I say or do things sometimes. I say things before I have thought about it but I try to be as non-judgmental as I can. I try to look outside the box at everything that is presented to me because as human beings deserve the time to be understood and heard and validated. Expectations when placed can make people feel trapped and confined to act and look a certain way this is simply not okay, I know this sound simple but within mental health and any illness it should not be so judged and making people feel like they don't belong. Be curious not dismissive.

A WAY OUT

Now I know what it feels like to feel and think that taking my life was a way out. I felt no one could help me that I was damaging society and my family. But also, to escape my trauma and escape reality. I was terrified of facing reality and scared of what the future would hold. I wasn't thinking about anyone but myself. I could not see the pain I was creating around me. The stress on my family and the people in my life. My mind became very narrow. When I attempted it only made things much worse. My suicidal thoughts became harder to fight which meant I was constantly acting on my urges each time I did this it became easier to withdraw from the world and more on acting upon urges it became such a vicious cycle. What someone goes through is valid we all think and feel situations differently. The way we deal with distress is not the same so please be mindful that when talking to someone with suicidal ideation that what they are feeling is genuine and raw. When people feel there is no way out of a situation sometimes, they withdraw completely and suddenly the impact can be horrific and as sad as it is it does happen. Suicide is something that is real and does happen I wish it didn't but does but if you're reading and you feel this way please reach out. if you have lost someone, I am so sorry you've had to experience losing them and those with chronic suicidal thoughts I am so proud that today at this time you are reading this because you will now know you're not alone.

Feeling alone

There is nothing worse than feeling alone. Feeling alone is a horrible feeling My experience is it can make each day as daunting and dark as the next. I felt my world was caving in because I could not bring myself to communicate with others in an healthy way which ended up me feeling more alone. Then the guilt and confrontation made me feel unheard this piled onto each other making me feel like I was the only one going through hardship which in theory I knew that was not the case but, in my mind, and how I felt it, felt so raw and real and it would constantly play on my mind. Then I struggled to communicate this by resorting in ways of hurting myself. People can sometimes withdraw when they feel alone because it can also come with the feeling of being a burden or an issue in others lives. Sometimes a cycle starts and it creates worse self-beliefs which communicates to the brain that you feel alone but realistically you're not alone it's a feeling not a fact. That's what trips people up the deeper they fall into this cycle the harder they find to get out of it. Creating this narrow tunnel view on the world and diminishes the relations the person does have. When people feel alone sometimes they can feel the interactions they do have are people attacking them. This is hard to stomach at first but let me explain. I myself have felt this way in the past. For me when suggestions are made sometimes I feel I am being judged and not heard, that people are angry with me this is because of situations in the past. I carry that trauma and self hatred with me and it impairs my judgement now. I don't do this on purpose but I assume the worse. Its almost easier sometimes to predict the situation in effort to not experience new events. You might think its silly but its real when you are going through it.

Thank you for staying on this journey with me. I hope so far that this has helped you gain some insight and to break the stigma of suicidal ideation.

Healthy coping skills

I am going to now share some skills I have learnt and been passed down for me to use. These are only a few of many skills, a tool, there are many more out there and not all of them will elevate your distress but I do hope you find it useful. Open up your mind and continue to be curious about these skills give them a go they maybe helpful or suggest them to loved ones. skills usually require repetitive action to help it form a habit. Healthy coping mechanisms require patience and sometime may require you to have assistance until you feel more comfortable doing them on your own and that is okay.

Opposite action

Opposite action is a dbt skill used to help challenge your thinking and to make healthier decisions that may challenge your emotions. To basically do the opposite of what your emotions are telling you. This can help create new pathways in the brain to react differently to what you would have done in the past. It also challenges you to do something different to be willing to stop a behavior you don't want to continue. Let's break it down. If you have urges think of what first comes into your mind. For me self-harming. I think what would I usually do next. Also think about recovery where you want to get to. It's also helpful to think of the consequences of that action. Now think of two things you could do that's opposite of what your emotions are telling you. For me I think of singing, art or talking to someone I trust. Then you need to pick one and commit to it. You may feel anxious, frustrated your urges may increase at the start but after the wave of emotions you should when practiced be able to have the urges pass or become less intense. Now it's important to remember that not all skills are helpful but its defiantly worth a shot. This skill in particular has helped my urges a great deal. Sometimes for me when I don't fully commit, I see myself falling back to old habits but when I use this skill with the right intention it does work.

Noticing

Being able to notice a behaviors or problem is the first step to being able to come to a wise mind decision. Being able to make a decision that will benefit your mental health and keep you safe. Noticing is not always easy as saying it. Noticing takes practice and it means reflecting sometimes painful parts of ourselves that we don't want to look at. This can be very challenging I will validate that. I suggest when using this skill notice smaller things first for example "I noticed the sun above me". Then work your way into things you would like to change. Things that may challenge you a bit but not to overwhelming. "today I didn't drink much water I notice it made me feel blah". This is noticing but also realize how its impacting me and what maybe I could do to not feel the way I am feeling. When you are ready you can start to acknowledge things within yourself that might make you react in a different way. I struggle with this a lot as it confronting but it does help me realize and more aware of my behaviors to try stop it before it happens. This skill allows a level of control back into my life and I am extremely grateful I have this in my tool kit.

Tip

Tip consist of putting your face into a towel of ice water holding for as long as you can you can do this multiple times. Doing quick exercise. Some examples are star jumps, push up. Anything that will get the heart rate going. Then squeezing muscles so making a fist squeeze tight let go and repeat you cand do different muscles. Ow some breathing. Best way to do this is in for four holds for four and out for four and do it four times. This skill help regulates the nervous system and immediately helps you re focus yourself. This skill when done right can help settle immediate urges or other symptoms, there is preparation required to do this skill. So that its ready for when you need it. Either making ice cubes or buying ice. I use reusable ice cubes as its easier for me to assemble. A towel for your face is helpful you can store. One by freezer so its ready with a bowl. For me this skill really allows me to reset and move forward it's not always pleasant to do it but I honestly benefit doing it. Sometimes I can be not wanting to do it but I know deep down the benefit outweighs the not doing it. This is where you can implement opposite action. By doing the opposite of emotions.

Sensory tools

Sensory tools are amazing they can aid us in so many was. Sensory meaning it uses the senses to help control anxieties and distress. The sense being smell taste what you can see, feel and hear. Few examples of smell citrus it awakes and can be a piercing smell to alert you. It aids to make you become in the moment. Smells like coffee or chocolate ore strawberries could be a calming smell to help you re gather yourself. You could associate smell with feeling safe sometimes that helps you to ground yourself. What we see. Looking at the beach and the waves or river stream, looking at the sky or your favorite place can help you to feel safe. Thins like fidget toys watching it work can slow the mind down. Things you can feel kinetic sand a rock or crystal feeling a pillow and how smooth it is and squishing fidget toy being able to. Focus the emotion into squeezing and realizing. These can shift the attention to the present moment which helps to bring you back into your body. Things we hear sounds of the ocean, music, white noise, nature sound can help us gather a safety net and allow us to feel safe but can also work as a distraction. These senses are individual you will need to try some in order to find what works for you what helps you and what will help you feel safer within yourself and surroundings

Skills don't always automatically fix a situation to become more in control of the situation you will need to balance skills and use them to help you work through the things you are struggling with. It will release feelings but not make them disappear our goal is to elevate distress in order to work through it and move forward.

Now as I come to the end of the book, I want to remind you that self-care is so important and that if you feel overwhelmed by this book please reach out to a friend or a loved one. Talk about it. I am very grateful to the person reading this as this shows in one way or another you want to help yourself or others become more aware of suicidal ideation that's a massive step, I acknowledge the time you have put in on reading this.

Acknowledgments

Tessa Harbutt

She has truly inspired me to be a better version of myself. I couldn't have written this book without her support. To me I will always look up to her she's help me to help myself and always treated me with respect and guidance. Thank you, Tessa, for the hours of showing me

I can be more than my illness I will be forever grateful. you are one amazing human being.

Melanie Strydom

Thank you for never being shy to tell me the truth. With the honesty, care, time I have the up most respect for you supporting me through this journey. You taught me about curiosity and its really changed my views on life. We share the same view on awareness and your feedback honestly helps me grow and challenges me. The work you do inspires me to help others and shows me anything is possible with hard work. Thank you so much.

hey my name is Charlotte aroha rameka. I am from Hawkes Bay New Zealand. I am the oldest of 8. I have struggled with my mental health most my life being diagnosed with clinical depression, complex post-traumatic stress disorder (cptsd), borderline personality disorder and chronic suicidality. I am still very much on the road to recovery and far from perfect but I have seen so many things and always kept my eyes wide open. I have encouraged myself to always be open minded and learn about the things I find challenging because I don't want to continue to be in the same cycle or place, I was in. I defiantly am one of those people who always have learnt the hard way because I am very stubborn and sometimes struggle with reality but I have grown a lot stronger in what I want for myself, who I want in my life and the fact I am still alive. But being human, I will still face some rough times ahead but I hope that my skills and determination will get me through. I feel extremely lucky being 24 because I still have so much to offer the world and I don't want someone to be in that dark hole I was. It is not always reality but if I can help someone by publishing this book, I would feel so humble that they took the time to read it. my next steps are to return to a treatment center Ashburn and focus on getting well and healing I am excited for that. But for the meantime I am going to focus on my therapy and sharing memories with my best friend and friends and enjoy each moment that arises and each challenge with the best of my ability to help myself. I wrote this book because I am so passionate about mental health and if something just something resonates with someone to help them then I am blessed. I know how it feels to be alone and I just want people to know that they are not alone that in fact there's someone who is fighting the battle beside them. My message is investing in yourself and give yourself a chance to live before doing anything that will be permanent because you deserve to be here. You are not a burden. You deserve to be in the world. You can make a difference too.